Why *Fear*
When Our Steps
Are *Ordered*

——————— *Darjisa Santiago* ———————

ISBN 978-1-63844-883-9 (paperback)
ISBN 978-1-63844-884-6 (digital)

Christian Faith Publishing, Inc.
832 Park Avenue
Meadville, PA 16335
www.christianfaithpublishing.com

Scripture quotations marked (KJV) are taken from the King James Version of the Holy Bible, public domain.

Scripture quotations marked (NLT) are taken from the Holy Bible, New Living Translation, copyright © 1996, 2004, 2007 by Tyndale House Foundation. Used by permission of Tyndale House Publishers, Inc., Carol Stream, IL 60188. All rights reserved.

Printed in the United States of America

*L*ife is short! Tomorrow is not promised! Some people are living in fear, unemployed, dealing with the loss of a loved one, not knowing where their next meal is going to come from, and some do not have anywhere to live due to evictions from this pandemic. All of these real-life situations are lived by many people today and witnessed by many social workers like myself and other frontline first responders daily.

It was during these unprecedented times that I was driven to refocus on what is important: family, friends, and taking the leap of faith to trust God now more than ever!

> For we walk by faith, not by sight. (2 Corinthians 5:7 KJV)

Those were some of thoughts that were at the forefront of my mind before hanging in my resignation at a state agency that I had worked with for seven years. Along with these other questions, I asked myself, "What are you waiting for? *Live your life*! What can I do to help be that positive change agent? Why should I fear when my steps are ordered by God!"

The thoughts of getting back to the basics reminded me of one of my childhood dreams, which were to inspire others to enjoy their journey and to live their best life ever today, and not to wait, which is why my dream was reignited.

In the following five short chapters, I want to share a glimpse of how my life began, and as I do, I pray that the seed of faith grows into what God has for you in your life...as it is being lived out for this girl from Far Rockaway, Queens.

> For I know the plans I have for you declares the Lord, plans to prosper you and not to harm you, plans to give you hope and a future. (Jeremiah 29:11 NLT)

Chapter 1 ───────

The Foundation

While growing up in Far Rockaway, Queens, with my Puerto Rican father and Dominican mother and two siblings, I remember looking out the window of our third-floor apartment near the beach, thinking and imagining a world waiting for me out there! As a middle child, I dreamed of being an advocate for others who could not help themselves and wanting to make a difference in a positive way in this world!

My parents raised us in a traditional Catholic Spanish home, where hard work and sacrifice was at the forefront of every decision in our household! They both worked together and sacrificed so much to make sure we had an education in a safe living environment.

After being in a public-school setting for about four years, from kindergarten to about the fourth grade, my mother took the leap of faith and enrolled us in a Catholic elementary school up until the eighth grade. After graduation, my sister and I attended a public high school—Beach Channel—while my brother attended a Catholic high school—Kellenberg—as my parents could not afford for all three of us to attend private high school. Despite the different types of education we received growing up, we were all able to graduate with our high school diploma.

My father worked full-time in a leather factory in the Bronx, while my mother cleaned houses part-time during the day to be available to take us to school in the morning and pick us up after school, which took place up until the eighth grade. My parents were not proficient in English, but that never stopped my mother from attending every parent-teacher meeting or my homecoming dance from the bleachers, which was embarrassing, but I remember it being the only way my sister and I being able to attend. The direct love and attention we received growing up was a bit controlling, but looking back, I can say it was our Spanish culture and a way of being protected.

During those early years, I remember many celebrations with immediate family members and close friends with our traditional Caribbean dishes—arroz con pollo (chicken and rice) and pastels (beef or chicken patties) with fried plantains. I also cherished those beach parties where we spent the whole day at the beach and my mother and aunt bringing us warm cooked meals at the beach shore.

My upbringing was sheltered from the outside world, but we had all the main ingredients that were demonstrated daily for us to live by according to Galatians 5: Fruits of the Spirit—love, joy, peace, patience, kindness, goodness, faithfulness, gentleness, and self-control.

My personal relationship with God became real for me when I started putting my faith/trust in him during the year of my independence, when I left my parents' home at the age of seventeen, since they did not agree with me wanting more freedom to hang out with friends and saving for a car. My parents taught me financial responsibility early when they started charging me monthly rent to live under their roof, which I did not agree with, so that is when I decided to move out and rent a room from a friend in Brooklyn, which was closer for me to attend Kingsborough Community College. My parents wanted me to concentrate on college and not get distracted with having a car or insurance payments.

During that time, I was working part-time in a clothing store and had saved enough money during the prior summer to be able to pay for a room and even purchase my first car—a Honda civic. Once I had my car and started attending Kingsborough Community College, I met a young man whom I thought was my "knight in shining armor," but boy was I wrong! We had a summer relationship, where we spent every day together and went to the park, beach, and house parties. Everything was going well until he started becoming controlling of me and not wanting me to be around my friends or family. At first, I told myself it was sweet how he cared for me and wanted to be around me all the time, but by then, it was too late. After that first slap across my face at a bus stop, I was in shock and cried and wanted to be alone. While being alone, I realized that my own father doesn't hit me, so why am I going to take this from a guy I just met! It took me about two months to file an order of protection and return home to my parents after finding out I was two months pregnant—at the age of eighteen.

What I remember during that time was my entire family giving me support, showing me what unconditional love looks like. I gave birth to my first baby boy at the age of nineteen, which was a blessing and truly made my relationship with my parents stronger. I remained home with my parents until my son was about six months old, when I decided to move out. My parents and siblings continued to help me with my son daily, weekly support as they would pick him up and drop him off at the babysitter who happened to be my godmother. The family support that I was given was everything to me during this time in my life. It showed me that I was not alone and that I was loved no matter what others might have thought of me or what I thought of myself. I remember thinking to myself, "I was not going to be a statistic—being a single mother on welfare." During this time, I was working at a clothing store part-time as I had to drop out of Kingsborough Community College after attending for one year.

My next step was to obtain a skill to support myself and my son, so I attended a trade school in New York City where I learned computer skills and how to type sixty-five words per minute. During that time in my life, I applied and received government assistance for rent and food, which I told myself would be temporary. I received the government assistance until my son turned two years old, when I graduated from the trade school, and was able to obtain a full-time position in a law office as an administrative assistant. Receiving government assistance did serve a purpose, and I am so grateful for the additional support to get me to my next step in life!

> Do not despise these small beginnings, for the
> Lord rejoices to see the work begin. (Zechariah
> 4:10 NLT)

No matter where you are right now in your life, I want to encourage you to keep going! Everything will make sense, don't give up!

> The steps of a good man are ordered by the Lord;
> and he delighted in his way. (Psalm 37:23 KJV)

Chapter 2

The Rededication

While working as an administrative assistant, I had a relationship with a young man who truly loved me and my son, but I was not ready for marriage nor ready to have another child. At twenty-one years old, I left that relationship and moved in with my sister temporarily while I obtained another place to live. As I searched for a place to live, I met another young man who also was looking for a place to live as well, so needless to say, we became really close and started dating, fell in love, moved in together, and married within two years. Although our relationship started off rather quickly and us not being fully committed toward one another, we both made a decision to continue with our relationship and make it work.

This is when I rededicated my life to Christ and started going to a Christian church regularly where I attended weekly Bible classes as well as couples counseling. The Bible classes and counseling taught me how to apply the Bible verses to my everyday living in love. This was the season of my life that I tried to understand what it meant to be that virtuous woman spoken about:

> A wife of noble character who can find? She is worth far more than rubies. Her husband has full confidence in her and lacks nothing of value. She brings him good, not harm, all the days of

her life. She selects wool and flax and works
with eager hands. She is like the merchant ships,
bringing her food from a far. She gets up while
it is still night; she provides food for her family.
(Proverbs 31:10–15 NLT)

My mother was the inspiration to me in being that good wife
who gracefully took care of my siblings and I when she took us to
school daily and conducted household chores while she worked outside of the home for five to six hours a day. My mother even found
time to attend night school to obtain her GED. My mother is a
strong woman who wore many hats and did so with so much love
toward us and others around her. My mother continues to be that
pillar of love and strength in my life in her golden years!

My second pregnancy kept me focused on motherhood and
being that role model of a wife that my mother had shown me to
be. Although, looking back at those early years of motherhood, I
can say my conversations with God were very detailed and direct. I
remember getting results with my prayers because I kept it simple. I
spoke from the heart and did not beat around the bush with fancy,
educated words. God hears us and truly knows our heart's desires
but wants us to ask and speak to him like a normal conversation
you would have with your friend who was in front of you or on the
telephone.

A Time for Everything: "There is a time for
everything, and a season for every activity under
the heavens: a time to be born and time to die, a
time to plant and a time to uproot, a time to kill
and a time to heal, a time to tear down and a time
to build up, a time to weep and a time to laugh,
a time to mourn and a time to dance, a time to
scatter stones and a time to gather them, a time
to embrace and a time to refrain from embrac-
ing." (Ecclesiastes 3–5 KJV)

My third pregnancy was a surprise for us but not for God as I truly thought I could not handle any more responsibilities. Having my third son made me slow down and apply everything I learned from my other two children. I was able to stay home with my third son for ten months while I breastfed him as I had strategically planned financially with my monthly contributions. Being in a two-income household, I understood the importance of being able to survive and maintain rent, food, car notes, and children's basic needs. I prided myself in being able to always contribute to the marriage. So being a parent and learning not to be so hard on myself and allow myself to make mistakes was a lesson I learned. For instance, I remember having scheduled days to do certain chores such as laundry, cleaning, and food shopping days, and if they weren't done on those days, it would shift my whole schedule. I also remember being anal about having to clean up the pots, pans, and dishes after preparing family meals—not leaving the kitchen a mess with dishes in the sink, which was hard for me as I learned later on in life that I was slightly OCD (obsessive-compulsive disorder). I recall being told, "We are not living in a museum, stop moving everything around." I still to this day cannot live in clutter!

After being unemployed for ten months and separated from my husband who remained working in the state of New York while I relocated to the state of Maryland was a difficult time to go through but necessary for me to be separated from my husband due to infidelity. I needed time to heal and be away from him to focus on being a mother of three and an individual. While finding full-time employment, which was not an easy task, it was another opportunity for me to rely on family supports again. My mother decided to move in with me and my three boys until she obtained her own place to live, which I was so grateful to have her in my life to help. It was during this time I remember having a desire to go back to college, and having my mother's support gave me the opportunity to take two classes at the local community college per semester as I had accumulated several credits from my first community college before having my first son. Obtaining my degree was always a goal of mine throughout the years that I kept striving for.

> I have been young, and now am old, yet I have not seen the righteous forsaken or his children begging for bread. (Psalm 37:25 KJV)

I recall attending community classes and still having time to read several inspirational books by Joyce Meyer, Joel Osteen, and T. D. Jakes as well as attend several women conferences such as "Women Thou Art Loose," which all contributed to my personal trusting relationship with my heavenly Father.

> Iron sharpens iron, so one man sharpens another. (Proverbs 27:17 NLT)

Having fellowship with others was a highlight to my week in those days. Just to be in the assembly of other believers gave me strength, along with praise and worship which would renew me and refresh my perspective. The best way I could explain it is how "recharged" I would feel when you do something you like…like getting a body massage or going for a walk to clear your thoughts or just taking a nap in the middle of the day—were all the good feelings I would feel in worship and fellowship!

> Not forsaking the assembling of ourselves together, as the manner of some is; but exhorting one another: and so much the more, as ye see the day approaching. (Hebrews 10:25 KJV)

Chapter 3

The Journey

*B*eing a mother, wife, and daughter were all different roles that were challenging at times to play out, but having positive role models around me helped me play my part in each scenario.

Motherhood for me is being able to demonstrate love freely to your children no matter what you expect them to do or not do. It is that unconditional love that was shown to me daily by my entire family and that I have been able to show my children. My mother's example of love shown in her cooking for us, taking us to school, doing house chores, taking us to church sure did rub off on me. I am so grateful to have been given the opportunity to experience first-hand what a loving, caring, God-fearing woman does for her family in good times and in bad times. My mother has always been the "glue that kept us together" throughout the years and continues to do so today. I thank God for her every day of my life!

My father is a hardworking man who continues to work odd jobs in his senior years. Although he is no longer in a relationship with my mother, they remain to be good friends. My father continues to participate in family events throughout the year with us all such as Thanksgiving, Christmas, and New Year's gatherings. My father has always been there for me; whenever I call on him, he has made himself available whether to give me advice about my boys or borrow money—he is just a phone call away.

Being a wife for me was an extension of what I saw my mother do with my father. At times there were good times and other times there were challenges to overcome, but through it all, I felt the love from both of my parents.

The challenges of being a wife for me were to stop trying to change the other person and learn how to forgive them and move on living in peace as much as possible.

As a daughter and having a loving, open relationship with both of my parents has truly been the foundation of why I am able to be open and honest with my three children today. Being a daughter taught me how to listen more and give less input, which has taken me years to learn. Sometimes being a supportive listener is all someone needs from us.

> My dear brothers and sisters, take note of this:
> Everyone should be quick to listen, slow to speak
> and slow to become angry. (James 1:19 NLT)

Chapter 4

Hitting Reset

*B*eing married for thirteen years taught me many valuable lessons, but the one I will focus on is how to forgive and to remember that none of us are perfect and that we are all a work in process, so don't be quick to judge the other person.

> Bear with each other and forgive one another
> if any of you has a grievance against someone.
> Forgive as the Lord forgave you. (Colossians 3:13
> NLT)

Although there were many happy moments, there were also some moments that I had to cry and look at myself in the mirror and self-talk myself into positivity because of betrayal and feeling alone. Now looking back at those moments, I can see how they build me into the person I am today—a caring, understanding, forgiving, empathetic individual. It was through all those difficult times that I learned how to seek God's face, peace, and grace even more. I remember praying the "Lord's Prayer":

> And forgive us our trespasses, as we forgive them
> that trespass against us. And lead us not into
> temptation but deliver us from evil. For thine is

the kingdom and the power and the glory forever. Amen. For if you forgive others their trespasses, your Heavenly Father will also forgive you. (Matthew 6:12–14 NLT)

Prayer consistently reminds me how our heavenly Father is perfect and how he came down to our human level to forgive us of our sins, so why would I not give other chances to be able to move in the right direction as our heavenly Father did.

Being divorced now for eleven years has brought relationships and prayer life to another level in my life. I am not resentful nor bitter of what challenges my marriage went through as now I able to speak from experience and encourage other women from my testimony of how he brough me through it.

God's favor combined with my faith has given me opportunities that only can be explained by his hand. For instance, I was offered a full scholarship while attending Arizona State University as long as I committed to work for the state agency for two years, which I agree to complete. Unbeknownst to me, that would start a career journey of seven years that would also offer me an opportunity to pursue my master's degree of social work. God knew my heart's desire and brought me to where I was! The importance of education was a desire that fueled me to want to do better! All those years of attending college classes part-time while I worked full-time and was mothering my three children paid off!

Let the favor of the Lord our God be upon us, and establish the work of our hands upon us; Yes, establish the work of our hands! (Psalm 90:17 NLT)

As the first college graduate in my family and being able to see how one of my sons achieved his dual associates degree in the general education curriculum and arts during this pandemic and how his hard work and dedication paid off are a blessing. As God provided for me during my educational journey, I have faith that he will do the same for my son as he was recently accepted into Arizona State University where he will pursue his master's degree in psychology.

> Be strong and courageous. Do not be afraid or terrified because of them for the Lord your God goes with you, he will never leave you nor forsake you. (Deuteronomy 31:6 NLT)

Keep dreaming, keep inspiring, keep being amazing right where you are!

God sees you and will reward you for your diligent work of excellence toward him not man! Stay the course as it will be worth it!

---------------------------- *Chapter 5* ----------------------------

Keep It Simple

*W*hat goes through your mind when someone says, "Keep it simple"?

For me, it's don't overthink it! If you don't understand what is being asked of you, then ask those follow-up questions for clarification. It will save you a lot of time with assuming what is being asked of you. Other suggestions that have worked in my life with keeping it simple is to try and remain positive in situations that you do not have any control over. Having that positive attitude truly does make a difference in how you approach tasks and lead others. We all have situations that we are going through, but it is how we go through them determines the outcome...changing your perspective does matter.

> Finally, brothers, whatever is true, whatever is honorable, whatever is just, whatever is pure, whatever is lovely, whatever is commendable, if there is any excellence, if there is anything worthy of praise, think about these things. (Philippians 4:8 KJV)

Having a good support system (your village of family and friends) through life's obstacles sure does help us all keep it simple as they refocus/shift our attention on what is important. Although I do understand that we go through various seasons in our lives, I also know that they won't last forever…according to Ecclesiastes:

> For everything there is a season, A time for every activity under heaven. A time to be born and a time to die. A time to plant and a time to harvest. A time to kill and a time to harvest. A time to kill and a time to heal. A time to tear down and a time to build up. A time to cry and a time to laugh. A time to grieve and a time to dance. A time to scatter stones and a time to gather stones. A time to embrace and a time to turn away. A time to search and a time to quit searching. A time to keep and a time to throw away. A time to tear and a time to mend. A time to be quiet and a time to speak. A time to love and a time to hate. A time for war and a time for peace. (Ecclesiastes 3:1–8 NLT)

Final Thoughts

*A*s the world continues to change around us daily, my prayer for you is to shift your focus on God, and lean on his promises through his word. To see how God has shown up time and time again in my life reassures me that he will do the same for you if you want him to. All you need to do is invite him into your heart and trust him with what he says according to *1 Chronicles 28:20*: "I will never leave you nor forsake you." God truly is no respecter of person, and if he is doing it for me, he can do it for you as well.

I encourage you to keep putting one foot in front of the other daily, knowing that you are not alone in this life. God, your sovereign father, is with you and cares about your family's well-being and yours. I employ you to trust his voice leading you to his perfect will as he continues to do in my life.

> He makes me to lie down in green pastures; He leads me beside the still waters. He restores my soul; He leads me in the paths of righteousness for his name's sake. (Psalm 23:2–3 KJV)

God has been my consistent source of peace and stability throughout my life. Although transition continues to happen in our lives, I have learned to trust in who holds me up as long as I remain connected and adaptable to the source, which is my heavenly Father. Having my focus on him will keep my mind off of the pandemic and focused on what truly is important—having a personal relationship with my heavenly Father who loves me, having a loving caring relationship with loved ones, and living out his/our dreams in this lifetime.

About the Author

*D*arjisa Santiago was born in the Bronx, New York, and raised in Far Rockaway, Queens, New York. Her parents are Puerto Rican and Dominican. Darjisa is the middle child of two siblings. She comes from a loving, supportive family who has always had her back! As a single mother of three handsome young man, she was able to be the first college graduate in her family to obtain her bachelor's and master's degree of social work, from Arizona State University. Her perseverance and dedication for education has ignited others to strive for their own accomplishments along her journey. Darjisa is known to be genuinely considerate and loving toward others. She loves and makes time with her family and friends. Darjisa has a type A personality, is very organized, and has integrity with a great work ethic. Darjisa enjoys outside activities such as hiking, going for walks, and reading inspirational books. She also loves to binge-watch series with her younger son. She is adaptable to change and enjoys new adventures. Darjisa aims to be remembered as a fragrance when she interacts with individuals instead of being remembered as an odor— because people will remember you, so it is up to you how you want to be remembered!

CPSIA information can be obtained
at www.ICGtesting.com
Printed in the USA
LVHW090531021121
702200LV00002B/350

9 781638 448839